P9-DEV-427

RISKY BUSINESS

Test Pilot

Taking Chances in the Air

By

KEITH ELLIOT GREENBERG

Featuring
photographs by Sergeant Pedro E. Ybañez, U.S. Air Force

A BLACKBIRCH PRESS BOOK

WOODBRIDGE, CONNECTICUT

Published by Blackbirch Press, Inc.
260 Amity Road
Woodbridge, CT 06525

©1997 Blackbirch Press, Inc.
First Edition

All rights reserved. No part of this book may be reproduced in any form without permission in writing from Blackbirch Press, Inc., except by a reviewer.

Printed in the United States

10 9 8 7 6 5 4 3 2 1

Special Thanks
The publisher would like to thank Colonel Jack Ivy and Major Rex Bailey of the United States Air Force for their invaluable help in putting this book together.

Library of Congress Cataloging-in-Publication Data

Greenberg, Keith Elliot.
    Test pilot/by Keith Elliot Greenberg.
        p.   cm. — (Risky business)
    Includes bibliographical references and index.
    Summary: Profiles the training and career of Major Rex Bailey, who tests military airplanes for the United States Air Force at Edwards Air Force Base in California.
    ISBN 1-56711-158-0 (lib. bdg. : alk. paper)
    1. Bailey, Rex—Juvenile literature. 2. Test pilots—United States—Biography—Juvenile literature. 3. Air pilots, Military—United States—Biography—Juvenile literature. [1. Bailey, Rex. 2. Test pilots. 3. Airplanes—Flight testing.] I. Title. II. Series: Risky business (Woodbridge, Conn.).
UG626.2.B25G74   1997
623.7'46048'092—dc20
[B]   95-38806
                                          CIP
                                          AC

There is a term in flying that is called "pushing the envelope." It means taking an airplane to its safety limits. Knowing background information about the aircraft is an important part of this. But the only way to truly understand an airplane's danger point involves getting in the air and taking it to the edge of possible disaster. That's what Major Rex Bailey does for the United States Air Force.

"We're here to give a new airplane to the Air Force," explains the 34-year-old test pilot. "It has to be safe. What I do is work the bugs out first, seeing what the airplane is capable of . . . pushing the envelope."

3

Major Rex Bailey does most of his work at Edwards Air Force Base in California.

Rex tests airplanes at Edwards Air Force Base in California's Mojave Desert, about 100 miles northeast of Los Angeles. The 65-square-mile base is filled with history. The first jet ever flown took off from there. Rockets were first developed on the grounds. Pilots, such as Chuck Yeager, first attempted to break the "speed of sound" at Edwards— flying a plane as quickly as it takes for sound to register in the human ear. Most of NASA's space shuttle flights currently land there.

Rex has dreamed of flying since he was a young boy.

The major has been preparing to fly since he was in the third grade. That's when young Rex first learned about the solar system at his Atlanta school, and American astronauts were getting ready to journey to the moon. On July 20, 1969, Rex sat in his grandfather's den with the rest of his family, watching history unfold on the screen of a black-and-white television. It was then that Neil Armstrong became the first man to walk on the moon. Rex decided that he wanted to be an astronaut, too.

Rex's job involves constant study and careful planning.

As time went on, he began considering other options. In the eleventh grade, Rex's mother—a chemist at the Nabisco cookie company—came home with material about the United States Air Force Academy in Colorado Springs, Colorado. This was a place where a young person could go to learn about airplanes. But getting in would not be easy. The entrance requirements called for candidates to be appointed by an elected official.

Rex and his co-pilot prepare to take a flight.

9

The Air Force trains pilots in math and science as part of their preparation for flying.

Rex paid a visit to the home of Lillian Carter, mother of Jimmy Carter, the president at the time. But, with so many other important issues demanding the president's attention, Lillian couldn't arrange for him to appoint the young man to the Air Force Academy.

Instead, Rex contacted a young politician named Newt Gingrich, then in his first year as a U. S. congressman. Gingrich, who became Speaker of the House in 1994, helped Rex get into the Academy in 1979.

A good test pilot learns how things move through the air, a science called aerodynamics.

11

After three years of training, Rex was finally allowed to operate an airplane in his senior year at the Academy. First, he and his instructor discussed the course he'd fly. Then, the two climbed into a T-41—a small, single-engine, propeller-driven plane—and took off.

As Rex looked down at the ground below him for the first time he said, "This is going to be fun."

In 1983, Rex graduated from the Academy with the rank of second lieutenant. The Air Force now sent him to Columbus, Mississippi, for jet-pilot training.

Rex gets ready to board a sleek F-16 jet fighter.

In Columbus, Rex flew two types of airplanes: the T-37 called "The Tweet" because its high-pitched engine sounds like the cartoon character Tweety Bird; and the T-38, an easy-to-maneuver aircraft also known as "The White Rocket."

Once jet-pilot training was over, Rex was sent to fly the KC-135, a tanker that refuels airplanes in the air. "We were like a flying gas station," Rex chuckles. "When you're fueling up another plane, the other pilot will get on the radio and joke, 'Can you check under the hood and fill up the tires?'"

A B-2 is refueled
in the air.

Rex checks his controls in
the cockpit of a B-2 Stealth
Bomber.

After flying the KC-135, Rex flew the FB-111. This is called a "swing wing fighter bomber" because the wings actually swing back, allowing the high-tech fighter plane to travel at two-and-a-half times the speed of sound.

"When you're high in the air, you don't really notice," Rex says. "But when you're close to the ground, you look down and see yourself flying by things at 11 miles a minute, 660 miles an hour . . . that's a real sensation."

Every move Rex makes in a plane is carefully mapped out in advance.

In 1991, after more training, Rex became one of the special few test pilots in the U.S. Air Force. "It's not as dangerous as it used to be," he says. "Thirty years ago, there were probably accidents every month. People would fly and not even know what their airplanes could do. The engines would blow up, and, sometimes, the wings fell off.

"Back in the 1940s and 1950s, guys would fly under bridges and do loops and rolls in the sky—whenever the mood struck them. Those days are long gone. Today, every move you do is planned out beforehand by the pilots, engineers, and management."

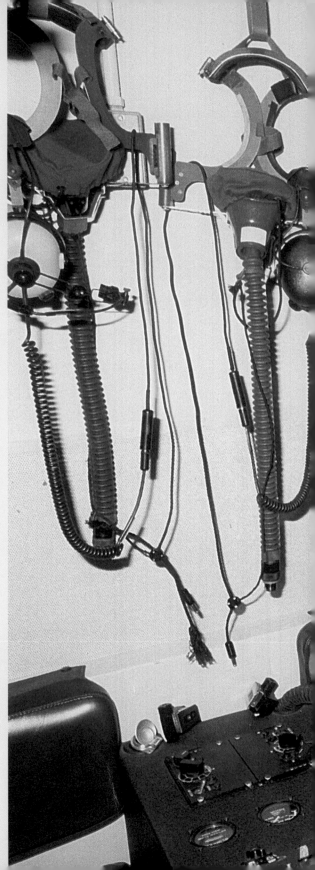

Before Rex gets into a new plane, he will experiment in a "simulator," a machine designed to reproduce the feeling of flying a particular aircraft. "It's like a full motion video game," he says. "You're seated in the cockpit, and there are video images of the runway, buildings, even cars on the highway and people on the ground. The cockpit shakes, like you're hitting turbulence. If somebody blindfolded you and brought you there, you'd really think you were in a real plane."

A fellow officer helps Rex with one of his many pre-flight simulations.

20

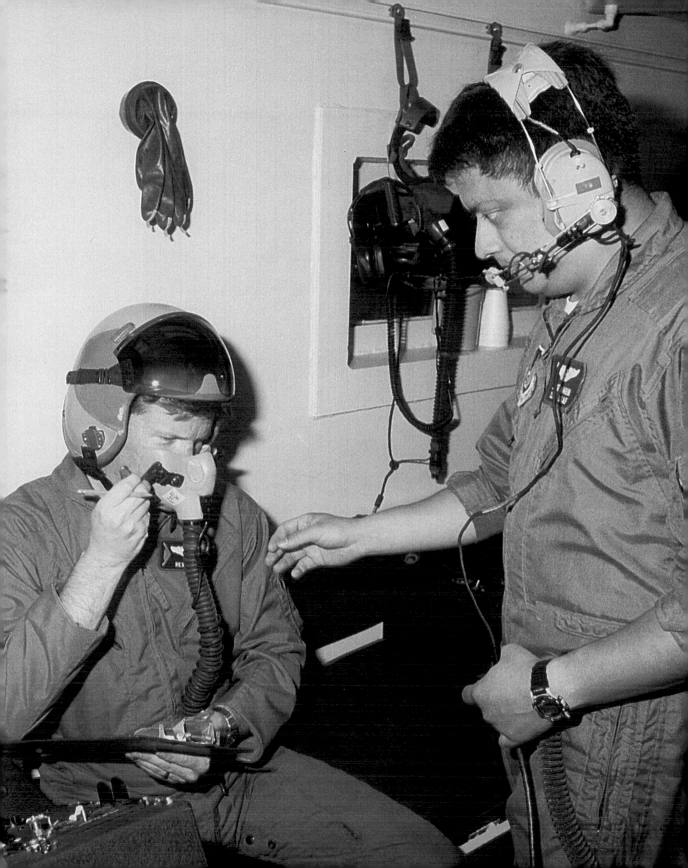

Despite these tests, there can still be problems once the actual plane is in the air. When trouble starts, Rex says, "you go back to where it's safe. You try to land." As a very last resort, a pilot may pull the "ejection handles," causing his or her seat to shoot out of the plane and parachute down to earth.

"We understand the airplanes well enough to take most of the surprises out," Rex says. "But when those surprises do come up, it's scary."

Test pilots must always discuss and understand every element of the planes they fly.

Rex double-checks the underside of a B-2 before taking it for a flight.

Every week, Rex is quizzed on various emergency procedures. Should a problem occur mid-flight, the survival methods are fresh in his mind.

Rex looks over his flying "card," which tells him exactly what he should do during the flight.

Every three years, Rex goes into an "altitude chamber." This is a special room without oxygen, with conditions that are similar to being in an airplane 35,000 feet in the air. He removes his oxygen mask and breathes—in order to determine what would occur if he lost oxygen in the middle of a flight.

On a day he is scheduled to fly, Rex attends a briefing with engineers, other pilots, and members of the team that guide the plane from the control room. They carefully go over everything Rex will do in the air. The final information is then printed on a card. Once in the air, the test pilot is expected to "fly the card," following the instructions from top to bottom.

About 90 minutes before takeoff, Rex walks around the airplane, looking for leaks or damage. Then, he enters the aircraft, turning on all the equipment, to confirm that everything works.

A typical test flight lasts between four and five hours. Rex either flies the B-2—the Stealth Bomber being tested by the Air Force—or the F-16. The F-16 is a single-seat fighter jet that is used as the "chase plane" during every test. It follows closely behind the B-2, reminding the pilot to always stay within the boundaries of Edwards Air Force Base.

Before takeoff, Rex will inspect the outside of his plane for leaks or damage.

Oxygen masks and helmets are important to pilots flying so high above the clouds.

The chase plane uses radar to check for other airplanes wandering into the vicinity and looks for any parts that may fall off the test plane at high speeds.

There are many tests that Rex tries with the B-2. In a "low altitude, terrain-following" flight, the pilot flies close to the ground, going up with every hill and down into every valley. The purpose of "performance testing" is to determine how high or fast an airplane will go. A "roll" involves banking an aircraft from one side to another.

Sometimes, Rex participates in an "icing test," where a B-2 flies up behind another airplane and sprays it with water.

A B-2 bomber prepares for takeoff.

The B-2, known as the Stealth Bomber, is the aircraft used in many of Rex's test flights.

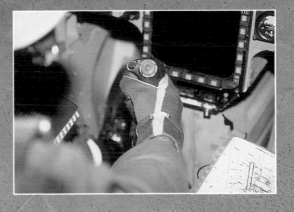

Because the aircraft is so high in the air, the water immediately freezes. The purpose of the test is to learn how well the plane can fly with ice on its body and wings.

29

Rex feels lucky
that he loves his
work so much.

Once a test flight is over, Rex checks the outside of the plane to make sure nothing has fallen off. Then, he goes into another meeting to discuss the test flight.

Rex doesn't fly every day. But even when he's home, on the ground, Rex is often thinking about airplanes. He admits that his career is not so much a job, but a great hobby.

"I would gladly pay money to do what I do," he says. "It's fun. It's an escape. There's a freedom about flying that I just can't put into words."

Above: Rex works on flight reports at home.
Below: The Bailey family includes young son Nicholas and wife Kim.

FURTHER READING

Bendick, Jeanne. *Eureka! It's an Airplane!* Brookfield, CT: Millbrook Press 1992.

Goodman, Mike. *Astronauts.* New York: Macmillan Children's Book Group, 1989.

Harris, Jack. *Test Pilots.* New York: Macmillan Children's Book Group, 1989.

Kerrod, Robin. *Amazing Flying Machines.* New York: Knopf Books for Young Readers, 1992.

Norman, C. J. *Combat Aircraft.* New York: Franklin Watts, 1986.

INDEX